I MET MURDER ON THE WAY

I met Murder on the way -

THE STORY OF THE PEARSONS OF COOLACREASE

Alan Stanley

Published by
The Author
Alan Stanley ©
Quinagh, Carlow
Co. Carlow

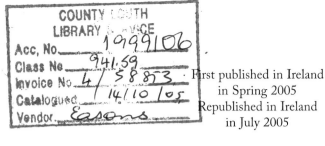
First published in Ireland
in Spring 2005
Republished in Ireland
in July 2005

by
The Author
Alan Stanley
Quinagh, Carlow
Co. Carlow

Printed by
The Leinster Leader Ltd.
Naas, Co. Kildare, Ireland

Copyright
Alan Stanley ©
Quinagh, Carlow

ISBN
0950175889

Designed by Derry Dillon

To the Pearson kindred everywhere for whom the memory of Richard and Abraham endures.

A.S.

ACKNOWLEDGEMENTS

I am grateful to Dr. John Feehan of Birr and Dr. John Carter of Ballyfin, both of whom responded generously to my importunate requests for a reading. Their pertinent responses and suggestions spurred me on to the finish.

For information concerning the fourteen Protestant men shot near Bandon in revenge for the death of an I.R.A. officer, I am indebted to Peter Hart's excellent history of *The IRA and its Enemies*, page 115, published by Clarendon Press. The same source, pages 302-304 provided information on Protestants as "spies and informers", and page 175 portrays the attitude of fathers to their sons' involvement with the I.R.A. I used all of these to illuminate my arguments.

For my description of the McMahon murders in North Belfast I acknowledge Marionne Elliott's history of *The Catholics of Ulster*, page 375, published by Penguin Press and *The Irish Civil War* by Tim Pat Coogan and George Morrison, page 40, published by The Orion Publishing Group.

For information on the four hundred and fifty-seven members of the Royal Irish Constabulary killed as a result of political violence between 1916 and 1922 I am indebted to Jim Herlihy's *Royal Irish Constabulary* page 152, published by Four Courts Press.

The photographs dating from 1921 and before were supplied courtesy of Mrs. Doris Turnnidge of Melbourne, daughter of Ethel Pearson. Doris also furnished a true copy of Mrs. Susan Pearson's death certificate on which is recorded the ages of the Pearson children.

Most of the information on the secretive fraternity known variously as Cooneyites, the no name church etc. was given generously by David Butler, from his notes and research for his up-coming book on dissenting Protestant sects in Ireland.

I am indebted to Mr. Paddy Heaney of Cadamstown who was able to confirm the time of day at which the armed confrontation, concerning the felled tree incident, took place.

The bulk of what passes as my own contribution was gleaned from the recollections of my late father, William Stanley. In a sense, his was a lifelong endeavour to come to terms with the upheaval that led to the establishment of the Irish Free State in general, and the tragedy of Coolacrease in particular. It was an honest endeavour, and one which, not infrequently, lured him down a dark and lonely path. I acknowledge his contribution.

My daughters Maeve and Ruth and my son Mike gave me much cheerful instruction in the use of the personal computer, to the point where I now claim a semi-literacy of the apparatus.

Catherine, my wife, checked for major grammatical _faux pas_. The errors that persist, however, are mine and mine alone.

As are my interpretations of the events depicted. Others will interpret differently and that is entirely their prerogative. _A. S. 2005_

FOREWORD

Coolacrease ruins seem always in shadow. The stones, laid bare by fire and weather, are haunted by the cruel deaths that happened there in June 1921.

Fifty-four years afterwards William (Willie) Stanley, slight, dignified and seventy-five years old, leaned against the mantelpiece in my living room and told me the story. As a historian I tend to listen to oral stories with healthy scepticism, and believe many old people remember selectively. However, I grew to respect Willie's innate kindness and his passionate concern for truth, and to know the events at Coolacrease seared his brain indelibly.

Willie's son Alan grew up hearing, perhaps too much, of Coolacrease. Had he heard less he might have brought his considerable historian's skills to bear on the story before now. Still, better late than never.

Much has been written about the War of Independence. However, for too long the criminal events spurning Pearse's plea against rebel inhumanity have been obscured. Only during the past two decades has a necessary and unapologetic perspective appeared in print. In this context, Alan's monograph with its poignant photographs is a valuable publication. We shall never recapture the past, and it is not for the historian to invent. Alan has brought a mature desire to look into the truth of Coolacrease and, before it faded into the mists of time, has revealed it as something much less than patriotic idealism. He may not win much affection - lack of reverence for sacred cows can cause resentment, and others may give a different and sanitised account of the same events - yet Alan has deployed original material from those with intimate knowledge of the sordid episode in June 1921, and has written a balanced work of historical illumination.

Jack Carter
September 2004

PREFACE

I met Murder on the way –

Percy Bysshe Shelley
The Mask of Anarchy (1819) II

INTRODUCTION

The ruin of Coolacrease house lies one mile north-east of the hamlet of Cadamstown in the County of Offaly, formerly King's County. When, groaning under the mass of its masonry, it looms into sight, a sombre and leaden aspect is revealed.

With the present owner's permission secured, one may savour the aura within its walls and the confines of the courtyard. The emanations are palpable, a melancholy desolation. Here in this place, the stones tell the story of a crime of unspeakable cruelty.

The crime was committed against a gentle and decent family of God-fearing and dissenting Protestants. Their only misdemeanour had been a recent dispute with some neighbours who claimed a "mass path" through their lands. The problem arose because of damage being caused to crops by people walking over them. The conflict had been resolved, typically, "the path having been given to those who claimed a passage through it." This is not surprising, for this was the family's way, their code, ever to turn the other cheek, to cherish neighbour and do good to all and sundry.

It was here at Coolacrease that on the 30th June 1921, a band of thirty, perhaps forty armed and masked men descended on the house, torched it, then in the courtyard shot the two eldest sons of the household, aged nineteen and twenty four. The shooting took place in the presence of family members. These were the mother of the two boys, their three sisters and youngest brother. Also present were two female cousins. The sisters were aged sixteen, twenty one and twenty three, the youngest brother fourteen. The older of the visiting cousins was twenty, the younger was a child of not more than eleven years of age.

The twelve e-mail letters contained here were relayed to Yvonne Pratt of Melbourne at various intervals between August 2003 and April 2004. They attempt to throw light on this harrowing affair and to answer, or more frequently to suggest answers to some of the questions posed. In particular, I hoped to propagate the seeds of unease. I wanted to show that, approaching a century later, it simply is not good enough to survey the ruin of Coolacrease and salve the collective conscience by mumbling the time-worn and treacherous mantra, "they were spies and informers who got their just desserts." The Pearsons were a kindly, trusting family, too much so one would have to say, for their own safety. Their treatment, at the hands of masked, faceless men of violence was undeserved and nefarious. In deference to the ordeal they suffered we should hold their memory dear.

I have made a few changes and updated additions to my original letters to Yvonne, for publication.

Yvonne and husband Jack are retired grandparents. Yvonne is a member of the A.I.G.S. (The Australian Institute of Genealogical Studies Inc). She does volunteer work for them, and is a contributor to their official magazine, *The Genealogist*. It was their interest in genealogy that first brought them into contact with Jack's distant relatives, who died violently in 1921. I responded to Yvonne's request for information, believing I could cover the events in a few short e-mail letters. During the compilation of the eighth letter it dawned on me that I was in the process of writing an abundant testament, something I had desired, but failed to achieve in the past. Here, in my correspondence with this safe and distant "Antipodean", who by her own admission, knew little of Irish history and less of Irish nationalism, I had, without realising it, shed my inhibitions. The ink flowed freely where previously, in my failed attempts, it had been staunched.

I raced off an electronic missive. Might I publish my/her letters and could I use her name in the publication? Back came the immediate response. "Go for it and best wishes, Yvonne and Jack."

Alan Stanley
September 2004

CHAPTER ONE

How appropriate that he, of all people, should bring it to my attention, my Australian brother in law, the most affable of men. He is Ernest Addie, married to my sister Hilary, and living in the State of Victoria since 1960. To them alone of our family went the privilege of knowing and loving that earlier generation of Pearsons, the survivors who suffered grievously at the hands of Irish Nationalists in June 1921.

On a family roots website a lady was seeking information regarding a shooting at Coolacrease in 1921. You are the one with the information, Earnest reminded me. And you have held a mirror to their lives for our benefit in the Northern Hemisphere, I prompted. The lady's *bona fides* should be checked first, Earnest said. I agreed.

I have no great affection for computers. My son conjured the "page". "Look", he said, "the lady's surname is the same as

Abraham's middle name. Abraham Pratt Pearson. I let it lie. A week passed and memory prompted. Wasn't Pratt the name on the distaff side? Susan Pearson, mother of Richard Henry and Abraham Pratt Pearson. I checked my notes and records in disarray, some going back to 1981. It was indeed the case. And so began my correspondence with Yvonne Pratt, who lives, with husband Jack, on the outskirts of Melbourne.

Laboriously, I typed out:

Yvonne,

I have information regarding the outrage at Coolacrease on the 30th June 1921, if you are still interested. Some domestic affairs are keeping me busy at the moment and my computer skills are limited, so please be patient when it comes to replies.

Regards,
Alan Stanley.

CHAPTER TWO

The alacrity of Yvonne's response left me in no doubt of her genuine interest. She warmly acknowledged my offer. In the meantime, while awaiting my response, she would make an alliance of patience and anticipation.

Yvonne,

Some background to begin with. My Grandfather, Henry Stanley and his brother William, in the company of a man called Pearson (an uncle of the boys who were murdered) went to Australia c. 1876. My grandfather and William returned nine years later when William's health began to fail. Some years after he arrived home William married and managed to father eleven children, so I reckon he made a reasonable recovery. Later, another brother

Robert, married a girl called Pearson, a cousin of the aforementioned.

While in Australia they were based in Geelong, in the state of Victoria. They worked as labourers, there was talk of work done on Ballaret railway station. There was also mention of rebuilding the outlaw Ned Kelly's hut, after the shoot out.

On the way home they heard the explorer, Henry Morton Stanley, speak at Capetown. My grandfather, who was illiterate, brought a mounted duck billed platypus, presumably to prove to the incredulous that he had been to the antipodes.

Early in 1921 my father had incurred the wrath of the rebel I.R.A. (Irish Republican Army) and was ordered to move out of his district in the Queen's County (Laois). Because of the longstanding friendship between the Stanley and Pearson families he went to hide, live and work at Coolacrease. His name was also William and he was aged twenty-one at this time. He was working in a hayfield with the two boys when it was surrounded by a rebel force of about forty men. He was light and fleet of foot and managed to make his escape in spite of being fired on. The two boys, who were heavily built, were apprehended immediately.

A mostly accurate account of the "Cadamstown

Tragedy" is contained in a newspaper (now defunct) called *The King's County Chronicle*, of Thursday, 7th July 1921. This was a Unionist paper, the Nationalist *Midland Tribune* containing an almost verbatim account. Facsimile copies are available by writing to the National Library of Ireland, Kildare Street, Dublin 2.

My next effort will be to transcribe the article for you, a time consuming task for me.

More, much more, later. Continue to be patient.

Regards,
Alan Stanley.

CHAPTER THREE

Hello Yvonne,

Here is the contemporary newspaper report I promised. "Parsonstown" was the name of the town now known as Birr in County Offaly. The former name of Offaly was "The King's County". They were interred in the adjoining burial grounds of Killermogh Anglican Church, close to the village of Ballacolla in the Queen's County.

The Queen's County is now called County Laois. This is to help you make locations, as I know you are consulting maps.

Extract from The King's County Chronicle, Parsonstown,
Thursday July 7th, 1921.

TWO YOUNG FARMERS SHOT AND HOUSE BURNED
THE SHOOTING WITNESSED BY MOTHER AND SISTERS

On Thursday evening last two young farmers named Richard Henry and Abraham Pratt Pearson were taken from their home at Coolacrease, Cadamstown and shot.

At least six rifle or revolver bullets penetrated the bodies of each of the brothers, who shortly afterwards succumbed to their wounds. The shooting was witnessed by their sisters and two other ladies.

Their residence, furniture, and out offices, as well as ricks of hay and straw were burned.

The deceased's father and a younger brother were absent from the home and did not learn of what had happened until the following morning.

Coolacrease House is situated about four miles from Kinnity and one and a third from Cadamstown.

FORTY ARMED MEN

On Thursday evening of last week, at about four o' clock, while the two men were making hay in a field about thirty yards from their residence at Coolacrease, Cadamstown, they were surrounded by about forty armed and masked men, who ordered them to go up to the house, which they did, closely followed by a number of the men. On arrival there the men directed the occupants to put up their hands, a command which was complied with.

It was intimated to the family that the house was to be burned, and a number of the party thereupon proceeded to search the rooms, breaking, it is alleged most of the furniture and other articles, including a piano. While the search was in progress (a *Chronicle* Representative was informed) one of the girls was held up and asked if there was any money in the house, to which she replied that there was not, so far as she knew. This evidently satisfied the interrogator, who then joined the main party. The members of which, the search having been completed - were making preparations for burning the house. Hay, sprinkled with petrol, was placed in various places. Meanwhile, Mrs. Pearson, who had fainted when the raiders arrived, was being attended to by her two sons, Richard and Abraham, who were endeavouring to restore her to consciousness.

SHOT IN YARD

What exactly happened after this is not quite clear,

but we learn that the two young men were brought out to the yard at the back of the house, and at least six bullets fired at each of them, the occupants of the house, including the boy's mother, three sisters, and two other ladies, cousins, who were visiting the Pearson family at the time, having experienced the dreadful ordeal of witnessing the shooting.

In an interview with our reporter, one of the Miss Pearsons stated that she had not had the remotest idea that her two brothers were going to be shot. "I knew they were going to burn the house," she said, "but I did not think there was going to be any shooting. Though I saw my two brothers being confronted by a number of armed men, who were speaking to them in the yard, I did not think for a moment that Dick and Abe would be shot, being under the impression that they were only being questioned or cautioned not to report or say anything about the burning."

PREPARING FOR FIRE

While the tragedy was being enacted in the yard, which is in full view of the house, arrangements for setting fire to the residence and everything it contained, were proceeding apace. The girls asked leave to remove their clothing and bicycles, and also to be allowed to go out of the house, but the latter request was refused until the last moment, when they were allowed to get some clothing, one of the girls being given a bicycle, which was, however, not her own, and almost useless. All the occupants of the house, Mrs. Susan Pearson, her three daughters, Misses Tilda, Ethyl, and Emma, and the two cousins, Misses Evelyn Pearson and Kitty Pratt, then came out on the road, and in a few minutes, witnessed the destruction of their home, from which bicycles and other articles had been removed by the raiders, who then decamped.

The family were now homeless and scantily clad, in a sparsely populated district, -- more than a mile from any human habitation, -- and in the small hours of the morning.

The demeanour of the men when they first arrived at the house showed excitement; they burst in the door with, it is presumed, the butt end of rifles.

NO REASON GIVEN

Asked if she could assign a reason for the tragic occurrence, this lady said "I asked them what was the reason for their action in burning the house, and one of them said he did not know. I pointed out that it was an extraordinary thing to burn a house without having any reason for so doing. The reply to this was: "Don't think we are doing this because you are Protestants. It is not being done on that account."

Continuing, she said: "There was some trouble about a pathway last year, but this was settled long ago, the path having been given to those who claimed a passage through it. I don't think that has anything to do with this occurrence."

The two men, with others of their family, had been attending the wedding festival, in Tipperary, of a relative on the day before their tragic deaths. Their father Mr. Wm. Pearson and a younger brother Sydney, had gone to the house of some friends on Thursday morning and did not know of the terrible happening until Friday morning, when they became aware of what had occurred.

At 7.30 p.m. on Thursday evening Dr. F. W. Woods, Kinnitty, was summoned to attend the injured men, one of whom (Richard) was dying. He dressed the wounds of both men and remained in attendance for over an hour, when a party of police arrived and had the wounded men removed to Birr Military Barracks, where Richard succumbed two hours later, and Abraham at 6 o' clock on the following morning. The family were brought to the house of a relative, Mrs. Odlum, at Newbridge Street, Birr, where they stayed for some days.

The residence which has been destroyed was a slated two-storey dwelling. A row of out-offices and ricks of hay and straw were also given to the flames, and totally destroyed. Richard Pearson was 24, and his brother,

Abraham, 19, both being unmarried. The farm on which they were working is an extensive one.

THE WOUNDS DESCRIBED

A military enquiry, in lieu of an inquest, was held at the Military Barracks, Birr, on Sunday morning of last week, at 11 o' clock, to investigate the cause of death. A "Chronicle" reporter was permitted to be present during the taking of medical evidence.

Dr. Frederick W. Woods, M.O., Kinnity, stated that on Thursday night a civilian called to his house and said that his presence was required at Coolacrease House, where two men had been shot. The messenger asked him to go at once, as one of the men was dying. He left immediately on his bicycle, and on arriving, found the two men on a mattress in a field. He first attended Richard Henry, who was in a dying condition, and then attended to the other man, Abraham. He treated the wounds of both men antiseptically. Richard seemed to have bled considerably, having superficial wounds in the left shoulder, right groin and right buttock, in addition to which there were several wounds in the back, one of which had probably penetrated the lung. He also found a wound in the left lower leg, also of a superficial nature. They might have been caused by rifle or revolver bullets, which, in his opinion, were fired at close range, the wounds being saturated with blood. He spent an hour and a half at the house, which he left at about 9.15 p.m. On his way home he met Dr. Morton, who also examined the wounds. Both of the men were then removed to the Military Barracks, where Richard Pearson died of his wounds about two hours after admission, and Abraham on the following morning. In his opinion the cause of death was shock and sudden haemorrhage, caused by gunshot wounds, the fatal shot having been that which entered the right groin.

The medical evidence in connection with the death of Abraham was identical. The remains were removed for interment to the family burial place at Ballacolla (Queen's County), on Sunday.

———————

I have copied faithfully, contradictions and all.

Regards,
Alan Stanley.

CHAPTER FOUR

Man that is born of a woman is of
few days, and full of trouble.

Job. Ch.14, v.1.

Yvonne and husband Jack have been trying to take it all in. Yes, Jack's people were related, on the distaff side (Mrs. Susan Pearson's maiden name was Pratt). They have been building a family tree. They enquire if any of the perpetrators were caught, if an inquest was held. I understand all too well. The searing contents of this testimony are not wholly absorbed at a single reading. Perhaps they are not realised at the twenty-first intake. I post an e-mail and point out, anew, that in lieu of an inquest, there was a military enquiry. The perpetrators were not caught.

Hello Yvonne,

In the ransacking of the house you will note that the raiders took "bicycles and other articles". One of the bicycles belonged to Mrs. Susan Pearson's twenty year old neice Kitty Pratt. Earlier she had cycled more than twenty miles of difficult, mountainous terrain from the village of Camross. She travelled to be with her cousins, but almost certainly in hope of keeping a tryst with a young man later that evening (more of this later). Her bicycle was brand new and of course she never saw it again.

The wedding which the two boys attended in Tipperary on the previous day celebrated the union between Edward Evans and Mary Jane Davis. It took place at Timoney Anglican Church some miles from Roscrea and close to Knock village. Today the church is known as Corbally.

I thought you might like to know that the bodies were brought by the military from Birr Barracks to Killermogh Church Yard, for burial the following Sunday morning 3ʳᵈ July, 1921. If I have measured correctly on the map it is a distance of about thirty-two miles. Their bodies were placed on an open topped "Crossley Tender", a military vehicle much in use at the time, and first operated during World War One. The late Mr. Wallace Stanley of Ballitore, Co. Kildare (distantly related to me), witnessed the burial. He told me he was about twelve years old and staying with relatives near Killermogh at the time. He attended Matins that morning and as the congregation left the building, two or three Crossley Tenders drew up sharply at the entrance gate. A number of armed soldiers jumped down and ran to take up positions around the perimeter wall of the adjoining graveyard. They had with them some bloodhounds and their drooling chops made an unpleasant impression on the young lad. The coffins were immediately removed and carried by soldiers to the already open grave. The only mourners he remembered were two tall fair young women, walking behind the coffins, weeping bitterly. The coffins were lowered at once and the graves filled directly. The military decamped immediately, taking the mourners with them. The whole affair lasted just minutes.

There was no religious display whatever. No prayers, priest or chaplain. Neither was there any military display such as a volley or salute or last post and reveille. I questioned him closely on this last point. The nationalist myth that they were "spies and informers" is so overwhelming that one is in danger of falling into that insidious trap. I think I should not omit to mention here that I have come upon a small number of the minority community who give the impression of being beguiled by the nationalist myth. Perhaps it stems from a conviction that decent ordinary Irish people could not carry out such a dreadful act unless there was a good and valid reason for so doing. "They brought it on themselves", I was told more than once. When I asked for elaboration I was confronted with only deafening silence. This is understandable. The majority of Irish people was and continues to be decent, generous humans. It is in their nature to be so.

The overwhelming sentiment of the minority community was, however, of a different order. It spoke of incomprehension, disbelief and a cruel hurt. It seemed to say that the _bona fides_ of decency and generosity had long since been accepted, that Scullaboge was a past aberration. What could possibly excuse a crime of this magnitude at this stage?

Some time later, I spoke to Mr. Richard Bailey of Granston, Ballacolla. He confirmed what Wallace Stanley had told me in all its detail. He also described the confusion and fear felt by the worshippers at what they had just witnessed as they came out of the church. They did not hang about and hurried home with heavy hearts.

Why were they interred in this manner? The family was religious and I assume that some sort of private funeral rite took place at Birr military barracks prior to the removal of the bodies. My informants told me the Pearsons were "Cooneyites", a dissenting Protestant sect, founded by one Edward Cooney. The sect had its beginnings in Co. Fermanagh in 1870. They were variously known as "The Nameless House Church" and the "Two-by-Twos". Most people I talked to referred to them as "Dippers". It should be said that the members of the sect never refer to themselves by any of the above names. On all official documents, census papers, birth and death certificates etc. they style themselves quite simply "Christian".

They are secretive in their ways, but I believe the following observations may not be amiss. As their name implies they are a "House Church" denomination and therefore have no use for church buildings. In spite of this their influence world-wide continues to expand. The emphasis is on piety. They practise adult and, therefore, "believer's" baptism. There is a similarity with their Baptist counterparts in that they practise total immersion at christening. I presume this is responsible for the sobriquet "Dipper". In other respects they may have similarities with the Quakers, and perhaps even with the American Amish community, but I have no hard information on this.

The "Christian Convention" is an important institution. It would appear to be a sort of "Annual General Meeting" at which baptisms are performed, marriages arranged and conducted (the latter only after a prior formal and legalised register office union), and so forth. We will hear more of this later.

The I.R.A. had made it clear to all funeral undertakers that any participation in the obsequies of their "enemies" would exact the extreme penalty. In this most heartrending way victim's relatives were frequently obliged to carry out interments themselves. Why just the two young women mourners, Matilda and Ethel? A boastful claim of the I.R.A. was that they did not make war on women, a boast, which, when it suited, could easily be set aside for their convenience. Violet Finnamore told me that her mother Kitty Pratt and Mrs. Susan Pearson accompanied the bodies to Killermogh but remained in the vehicle while they were being interred.

I believe that what I have just told you belies utterly the notion that they were "spies and informers", as perpetrated by the nationalist myth. No country or power on earth recognizes its spies when they are exposed. A variant of the myth suggests that they were actively engaged, on the side of the authorities, against rebels. If this had been the case, some form of military display would have been evident.

I have been asked, frequently, why it was that these two dissenting Protestant boys were interred in the burial grounds of Killermogh Anglican Church. I do not have the answer to this question, and can only speculate as follows. Some of the old people told me, in 1981, they thought the family had come from that area, from the townland of Ballygeehan before moving to Cadamstown (The Christian Convention, referred to later in chapter six, see "Pearson Testament", took place close by in Carrick House). Killermogh was the boyhood parish of Henry Stanley, and he was already in possession of a burial plot there. In 1921, the only inhumation was Jane, Henry's wife, who died in 1919, so that much space remained. The very close proximity of the Pearson burial place, a mere few feet, with that of my own family's, causes me to wonder if Henry, for expediency, made his plot available. In 1981 I checked the official record of interments for Killermogh Church. No record of the interment of Dick and Abe Pearson had been made. I asked the incumbent to rectify the matter, giving him all details.

I should, perhaps, point out that in this "Police War", as the British called it, the military provided security only. They never went on the offensive.

Regards,

Alan.

CHAPTER FIVE

Through the jungle very softly flits a
A shadow and a sigh –
He is fear, Oh little Hunter, He is Fear!

Kipling.

Hello Yvonne,

After my father died on the 10th March 1981, and for a few years afterwards, I made enquiries about the affair, as I thought he might have withheld some information. I now know that this was not the case. His account seems to have been accurate in all its detail.

He told me that shortly before the tragedy and while William Pearson Snr. was absent, a group of rebels sawed down a tree on Pearson lands in order to create a barrier on the road. Richard challenged these people but they warned him off, making dire threats as to what would happen should he attempt to interfere. My father said Dick was somewhat hotheaded and further antagonised the intruders by trading words. "Aren't you the brave fellows with all your guns?" he admonished. In any event he went back to the house, retrieved a shotgun and discharged it over the heads of the rebels. The family would have been required to hand in their weapons and shotguns, to the authorities, and we can assume that this was done. A nationalist source claims that the I.R.A. also relieved the household of some weaponry. I think we must assume a gun was kept hidden out of sight for the control of vermin, but almost certainly, in these troubled times, with protection in mind. The firing of a shot over the heads of intruders had been a common enough response in the past, but foolhardy in the conditions that prevailed at this time. Had William Pearson snr. been at home, no doubt, wiser counsel would have prevailed.

My father said that early on the morning of the tragedy the postman came to deliver the mail. He secretly warned Mrs. Susan Pearson of what was about to take place. My father's version was that William Pearson Snr. was again absent on this occasion. The postman admitted his I.R.A. membership and said he had attended a meeting at which the decision had been made to kill Richard, Abe and my father. He said he was warning them because he had no stomach for the taking of innocent lives.

A family conference was held and tragically it was decided that this was a ruse to frighten the family from their property so that others could take possession. From the newspapers of the day they would have been aware of similar outrages around the country, particularly in west Cork. Here again my father felt, in retrospect, had Pearson Snr. been at home, wiser counsel might have prevailed.

My father was uneasy, and kept his eyes peeled, while working in the hay-field. He was first to see the gunmen approach and shouted to the two boys to run. My father was light and fleet of foot. They, on the other hand, were strong and heavily built. My father shouted a second time "run for your lives" but to no avail. He managed, as he ran for his life, to catch a last glimpse of them, as they stood rooted to the spot with their arms raised in the air. The field sloped downwards away from the gunmen and at the end was a low hedgerow over which my father vaulted to a steeper landing on the other side. He then ran alongside this hedge using it as cover, as up to a dozen gunmen took chase, but these he outdistanced with ease. In the course of his flight down the field, at least ten shots were aimed but only one made contact, causing a superficial scratch. He ran for many miles across country anxious not to draw attention to himself, as everywhere there were sympathisers to the rebel cause. He was on his feet as darkness fell and stumbled into a ditch or dyke. He was exhausted and fell asleep for a few hours. He was awakened by the cold, for while it was high summer, the night out of doors was much colder. To add to his discomfort, his coat had been left behind in the hayfield.

He did not know the terrain well, he was still avoiding the road, and as darkness fell, he wandered aimlessly. His objective was to find refuge in Tullamore, and presently he stumbled on a landmark, which he knew to be within striking distance of the house of a family called Bryant, friends of the Pearsons. He also knew that their abode, in the townland of Cloncon was just over a mile distant from Tullamore, his ultimate goal. My father too had befriended a young man of the house, Tommy, who was of similar age. He arrived after midnight to find the house locked and in darkness. He knocked loudly, hopeful they would take him in. Mr Bryant Snr. opened an upstairs window and in a voice that was barely more than a whisper called out "Who's there?" My father identified himself and then asked "What happened at the Pearsons?" The old man replied "Oh, it's too bad, it's too bad." My father told me he understood that the Bryants were too terrified to take him in and so he asked if he could have a coat as he was feeling the cold very acutely. A coat belonging to Tommy was secured and dropped to him from the window. My father again asked "What happened at the Pearsons?" The old man made the same reply. "Oh, it's too bad, it's too bad."

Tommy Bryant's daughter told me recently that earlier in the evening her father was preparing to cycle over to Coolacrease to enjoy an evening's socialising with the Pearson brothers, their elegant sisters and my father, but especially it seems he wished to keep a tryst with Kitty Pratt. Kitty's daughter, Violet Finnamore, told me that at this stage he had made her a gift of jewellery. A neighbour hurried in and said "Don't go, there's been trouble."

My father now intended walking to Tullamore to seek refuge in the R.I.C. (Royal Irish Constabulary) barracks. He continued to avoid the highway as he did not wish to draw attention to himself. He was by this stage weakened and confused and somewhere, on route, he was fascinated to see in the darkness a circle of faint lights. These were the cigarettes of a detachment of armed rebels who immediately apprehended him. They questioned him closely and held him blindfolded. He believed his captivity extended to two days. I have reason to believe that he was held for somewhat less than twenty-four hours and that he had become confused and disorientated through exhaustion and being blindfolded. He did not give his own name, but that of a Catholic cousin, named Carter (more likely to sympathise with the rebels), and this seems to have saved him. He spoke of the two guards which at different times were set over him. The first was rough, uncouth and threatening, and did nothing to relieve his apprehension. In contrast, the second was well spoken, showing a few small kindnesses and proffering cigarettes. My father speculated that he might have been a medical student.

The detachment was moving constantly and after some excitement when it seemed likely there might be an engagement with crown forces, they tied him to a tree and told him that if he moved he would be shot. They then decamped and after a long silence my father tried his knots. They were loosely tied, deliberately to facilitate his escape, and he freed himself easily. He was now many miles further from Tullamore than when he had started out. He eventually staggered up to the Barracks in the early hours of the following morning, and when a policeman opened the door, he collapsed.

Bye for now. More to follow when I get time.

Alan.

CHAPTER SIX

...a time to hate;
a time of war...

Ecclesiastes Ch. 3 V. 8.

Hello Yvonne,

Sorry for the long absence.

The killing of the two Pearson boys by the I.R.A. was replicated in many parts of the country at that time and particularly in the largest county, Cork. Their spokespeople insist that they are not sectarian but clearly they were then, and remain so. For instance, in 1922, with civil war looming, a local commander was ambushed and killed in Cork, almost certainly by some of his own people. His companions reasoned as follows. No one knew his movements, so his position was given away by "spies and informers". Protestants favoured the union with England, Scotland and Wales and were therefore likely to act as fifth columnists, spies etc. They immediately rounded up fourteen Protestant males of all ages, and shot them dead. Historians have ascertained that Protestants, for dread of the consequences, were loathe to give information to the authorities, and the information that did flow was much more likely to come from Catholics.

A book, published by the Oxford Press, entitled *The IRA and its Enemies*, gives an accurate insight into the period. The author is Peter Hart.

What follows is a transcription of two letters in my possession. The writers of both are deceased. Neither letter is dated but I have noted that both were written in the spring of 1983, i.e., March or thereabouts. The first was written by a Mr. Hogg, who was a retired Priest of the Anglican Church in Ireland. He was wary of my first enquiry and it needed a more robust statement of my *bona fides* to bring forth a response. The second is the testament of Dave Pearson, the youngest of the Pearson brothers who was close to his fifteenth birthday at the time of the tragedy. By 1981 he was a retired farmer living in Packenham in the state of Victoria. My sister, Hilary and her husband had made his acquaintance soon after they went to Australia in 1960, and maintained a friendship until his death. I felt it was important that an account of the terrible events should be recorded by a member of the family. I asked Hilary if she would approach Dave to do so. In a letter to me, dated 21st September 1981, Hilary describes the moment she broached the awkward subject. Dave and his wife Kathleen were guests in her house. He was quite taken aback. He was fearful of naming names. "These people would follow you to the ends of the earth", he said. He would talk it over with his older brother Sid and then decide. Sid was eighty years of age at that time, Dave was seventy five. I had sent Hilary a copy of *The King's County Chronicle* report to give to Dave. He was quite excited about that and would study it in detail, later, with the aid of his magnifying glass.

Hogg letter

Sunnyhome,
Love lane,
Tramore,
Co. Waterford.

Dear Mr. Stanley,

       I now appreciate your interest in the murders of the two fine young Pearson boys in 1921 as your late father was the one who succeeded in escaping the same fate. This was something which I do remember hearing about but I never heard his name mentioned so it must have been kept a great secret at the time. Now about your questions: Yes, my parents were very great friends of the Pearson family and my father was ex R. I.C. (Royal Irish Constabulary) sergeant, stationed in Clonaslee. Retired in 1918/19, bought a small farm near Kinnity for retirement. So this would be the R.I.C. connection which would not fit in with your information re. the young man named Hogg visiting the house previous to the tragedy. Someway I don't think our friendship with the family had any bearing on the motive for the murders. As I mentioned in my previous letter there were many burnings of Protestant homes and murders at the time so those who escaped were fortunate. All Protestants were suspect of giving information and loyalty to British rule as well as big owners of land (which was at the end of the troubles divided). This all happened of which you are very well aware and Protestants are now only 3% of the population of the republic. This is my summing up of the situation after 50 years of Independence. Please don't feel that I am a pessimist because of our sad history. I still have enough faith to believe the Church of Ireland (Anglican) will survive because we have some great young people who still care. This fills me with hope for the future.

I don't wish to carry on any further correspondence on the awful tragedy which I know upset my Parents greatly and even myself still when I hear it mentioned.

Thank you for your good wishes.

Yours sincerely,
G. S. Hogg.

Pearson Testament.

62, Ahern Road,
Packenham.

Dear Hilary,

In ref. to your brother's letter, to you, he wants to know why we were subjected to such treatment, at the hands of the I.R.A. A Roman Catholic man from Cadamstown (J. White), told us that the I.R.A. had allotted a quota for each district, to be eliminated, by a certain date. This may have applied to us.

Let us go back to that fatal [*sic*] day, the postman called with the mail. My mother received the mail, and was told by him that he had attended an I.R.A meeting the previous night, where they decided that my three brothers and father were to be shot that day. It had been arranged that my father and brother Syd were to go to a Christian Convention that day, which was held at "Carrick House". After a family conference they decided to go, as they felt they had done nothing to provoke the I.R.A. Your father and my two brothers and myself went to the hay paddock, to make hay. At approximately 11a.m. a man by the name of Hoban or Honen, arrived in the hay paddock and asked us if we had seen his horses, which had strayed. In actual fact, this was to pinpoint our position. We then went home and had lunch, returning to the field to continue hay-making.

At approx. 2-20 p.m. about 40 armed men burst into the paddock firing as [they] ran towards us. Your father ran, and eleven men followed him until they ran out of ammunition. The other members of the I.R.A. marched us home, where another contingent was going through the house throwing petrol around. After placing us in the boiler room, under armed guard, they proceeded to fire into the tractor. We were then brought out of the boiler-room, my two brothers were told that they had been sentenced to death the previous night. My Mother and three sisters and myself were ordered to go to the outside yard. My two brothers were stood against the barn wall, and shot by nineteen armed rebels, they then left, at approximately 4 p.m. I then rode on push-bike to Tullamore Barracks to raise the alarm. The military and Police put me into a Crossley Tender and a convoy of Military and Police took me back to Cadamstown, when we arrived there the authorities from Birr had taken the boys to Birr Hospital, where they died after admittance. The Rebels came back next day and stole cattle, horses, and harness. We were then taken into protective custody at Birr Military Barracks, where we stayed until the Truce was signed. My brother Syd went to live in England with your people. We then lived in the coach house on the farm and were often intimidated by rebels marching through the ruins with revolvers drawn. As regards your query about us giving information to the military, nothing could be further from the truth. If so why didn't my father and brothers pass on the information we had received from the postman that day. On this point our conscience is clear. Your father was correct in saying they were murdered for no reason. Your Grandfather was a great friend of my father's family for many years.

When Syd came back to the farm 12 months later and started ploughing, next morning he found a note on the plough, advising him to stop, or he would be shot. So it is evident their main object was to take over our land.

After 62 years I would like to forget this sordid affair. Hoping this information will be of value.

Yours Sincerely,
D. Pearson.

You will probably note that in previous correspondence I indicated my father had told me that Wm. Pearson Snr. was not present on the morning of the tragedy. Violet Fillamore concurs, saying that William Pearson and his son Sidney cycled to Carrick House, a distance of about about thirty-four miles, arriving the evening before in order to be fresh for the days business on the morrow.

In fixing the time of departure of the raiders at about 4 p.m. Dave gives us a clearer idea of the length of time it took Dick and Abe to die. It is reasonable to assume the shootings took place at 3.45 p.m. approximately. From *The King's County Chronicle* report we know Dr. Woods left Kinnity at 7.30 p.m. to cycle the five miles to Coolacrease, arriving at, say, 8 p.m. earliest. He remained one hour, till 9 p.m. when the police, presumably with the assistance of military Crossley Tenders, removed them to Birr, a journey of at least thirty minutes duration. Richard died two hours later, bringing us to 11.30 p.m. Abraham died at 6.00 a.m. the following morning.

The period of agony and struggle for Richard, therefore, extended to seven hours forty five minutes minimum and for Abraham to fourteen hours fifteen minutes.

The hospital Dave refers to was the military infirmary attached to the garrison at Crinkill, Birr where over one thousand soldiers were billeted.

Dave had to cycle to Tullamore, a distance of about thirteen miles because the I.R.A. had burned down the R.I.C. barracks in Kinnity, four miles away, on the 4th August 1920.

Kind regards,

Alan.

CHAPTER SEVEN

Hello Yvonne,

Here are some photographs, all I have been able to muster.

Kind regards,
Alan.

Coolacrease House in happier days.

A remarkable vernacular five bay abode constructed on a large scale (note the distance of window insets from corner).

In front of the ruin of Coolacrease House.

Beginning of July 1921.

(From left) Emily, Matilda, their father, William Pearson,
David and Ethel.

The ruin of Coolacrease House from the rear.
Beginning of July 1921.
(Note the dog cart and weighing scales left foreground).

In front of the ruin of Coolacrease House.

Beginning of July 1921.

Ethel, Matilda, Emily, Dave and their father William Pearson. The family dog seems unscathed. Perhaps the "practically useless" bicycle propped near the front door.

Mrs. Susan Pearson.

In the morning she misconstrued the warning of the man who tried to save them. In the course of the afternoon she saw her home burned. Then, in the courtyard, with her daughters, youngest son and two young nieces clutched about her, saw a firing party shoot dumdum rounds into her two eldest sons. After the raiders decamped, when Dave had set off for Tullamore, with flames raging about them, they carried the mortally wounded Dick and Abe, two tall heavy lads, out to the adjoining field and laid them on a mattress.

Group photographed at Coolacrease shortly before the shooting.

(From left) Ethel, Matilda, Emily and David Pearson, William Stanley, Sidney Pearson and Abraham Pearson (right), the younger of the two brothers, at nineteen years, who was shot.

The child (front) is a cousin, Evelyn Pearson, who with another young cousin, Kitty Pratt, saw the shooting of the brothers.

(As with some of the other photographs, frequent reproduction makes for poor copy).

William Pearson Snr.

Father of Richard, Matilda, Ethel, Abraham, Emily and David. He was absent with Sidney, at a "Christian Convention" held at Carrig House in a neighbouring county, on the day of the shootings.

Matilda Pearson (Tilly).

July 1921

Oldest of the girls at twenty three, (only Richard was older.) Saw her home burned and her two brothers shot. Immediately prior to the shooting she asked the raiders "What was the reason for their action in burning the house?"

Ethel Pearson.

July 1921, aged twenty one.

Saw her home burned and her two brothers shot. In old age, suffering dementia, she fixed padlocks to her doors.

Richard Pearson.
The older of the two boys, at twenty-four years, who was shot.

Emily Pearson (Emma).
July 1921, aged sixteen.
Saw her home burned and her two brothers shot. In 1951 she wrote a "wonderful" letter to William Stanley.

David Pearson (Dave).
July 1921.
His fifteenth birthday occurred on the 2nd. Saw his home burned and his two brothers shot. He then cycled thirteen miles to Tullamore to raise the alarm.

Sidney Pearson.
On holiday in Ireland, 1975.

Dave Pearson.
On holiday in Ireland, 1975.

View in Courtyard showing barn wall and arch leading to field.

"...in full view of the house."

This photograph was taken from a rear window ope of the ruined farmhouse. Dick and Abe were made to stand against the barn wall, on the far side of the vertical steel girder, before being shot. The view through the arch, by way of the tubular steel gate, is of the field where Dr. Woods found them lying, fatally wounded, on a matress.

William Stanley.

From a photograph taken in 1926.

View of graves.

Two diminutive Pearson family headstones. (Right foreground). In front, a family member, Ernest, died 1929 .
Richard and Abraham (behind, left), interred 3rd July 1921. Date of death is not recorded.

The caption reads:

>   Richard Henry Pearson
>   *Aged 24 years*
>   Abraham Pratt Pearson
>   *Aged 19 years*
>   *"Always Remembered"*

Richard's demise occurred on 30th June 1921, Abraham's on 1st July 1921. Close by, left, is the Stanley family plot.
(A closeness perpetuated.)

Overleaf **Reprint of true copy of Mrs. Susan Pearson's death certificate.**

THIRD SCHEDULE.

DEATHS in the District of *FRANKSTON* in
Victoria, Registered by *P.F.C. HOSKING.*

18444

1	1542
Description— 2.(1) When and where Died	16th May 1947 Community Hospital Frankston Shire of Frankston and Hastings County of Mornington
(2) Usual Place of Residence	12 King George Avenue Mornington
3 Name and Surname ... Occupation	Susan PEARSON Home Duties
4 Sex and Age	Female 76 years
5 (1) Cause of Death (2) Duration of last Illness	Cardiac Failure 1 month Hypostatic Pneumonia 5 days
(3) Legally qualified medical practitioner by whom certified ... and	Dr C.M. Hopkin...
(4) When he last saw Deceased...	15th May 1947
6 Name and surname of Father and Mother (maiden ... known), with Occupation	Henry PRATT Farmer Susan PRATT formerly EVANS
7 Signature, Description, and Residence of Informant ...	N.S. Muir 101 Main St Mornington Authorised agent
8 (1) Signature of Registrar (2) Date and (3) Where Registered ...	J.H.C. Hosking 17th May 1947 Frankston
If burial registered— 9 When and where Buried Undertaker by whom certified	19th May 1947 Mornington N.S. Muir Mornington
10 Name and Religion of Minister, or names of Witnesses of burial...	J.F. Jones Christian Assemblies of Australia.
11 Where born, and how long in the Australian States, stating which	Queen's County Ireland 18 years in Victoria
If deceased was married— 12 (1) Where and (2) At what Age and (3) To Whom... (4) Conjugal Condition at Date of Death	Ireland 24 years William PEARSON Widow
13 Issue in order of Birth, the Names and Ages	Richard Henry Deceased Susan Matilda 49 years Ethel May 47 years William Sydney 45 years Abraham Pratt Deceased Emma 41 years David 40 years

Coolacrease House in ruin.

June 2004.

"...the lush pastures of Ireland."

CHAPTER EIGHT

The illusions that sustain
us crumble slowly...
Shostakovich

Yvonne writes to ask if I can furnish more information on the Irish Republican Army, their *raison d'etre,* aims, motives etc. I fudge the questions and recommend instead that she consult the reading matter of people who are more competent than I am to supply answers. In particular I urge her again to read Peter Hart's history of *The IRA and its Enemies* which I mentioned earlier. For a view from a leading member of the I.R.A. during the war of independence and on the rebel side during the civil war, I recommend Ernest O' Malley and his accounts for both - *On Another Mans Wounds* and *The Singing*

Flame. These are extraordinary works told with consumate literary skill and a fine lyricism.

Hello Yvonne,

My father died in 1981 and the following year I had conversations with a few elderly people, fully *compos mentis*, who were "close to the affair" as young men. My principal informant was a Mr. Tom Mitchell who lived from childhood in the village of Kinnity, four miles from Cadamstown. I gained a few insights which I think are worth mentioning. It appears that Coolacrease had been put up for sale by its previous owners, people called Benwell, as recently as 1912 or thereabouts. People speculated that such a large holding (in Irish terms), would be purchased by the Irish Land Commission, whose business was overseeing the transfer of the freehold of land from landlord to tenant, or in this case, the distribution of the Benwell farm, in portions, among neighbouring small holders. For whatever reason, perhaps lack of funds, this did not happen. It was further believed that a number of people was bitterly disappointed, and consequently saw the new owners, the Pearsons, as interlopers. In the end, of course, the Land Commission, under the new Irish Government, did take control and in what amounted to an *uti possidetis*, vested the freehold in the peoples who had moved in on the lands, which were then paid for by way of annuities spread over 40 or 50 years.

I asked Tom Mitchell if anything was known of the postman who would have been delivering mail to Coolacrease at the time of the tragedy. Without hesitation, he said yes, that he was alive, alert and healthy in 1981. Would Mr. Mitchell be prepared to give me his name? This time there was a hesitation, some prompting, before, eventually, the name "Delahunty" was spoken. Might he be approachable? No, he was wary of strangers. I should not attempt it. I have since regretted taking that piece of advice. The most I could have suffered was a rebuttal. About this time, too, a friend was able to make a "proxy" enquiry on my behalf. Once again, the name uttered was Delahunty.

A cousin of my fathers, Oliver Stanley, told me that after the tree had been felled, a number of men came to man the barricade thus created, and were shortly afterwards surprised by security people (police and auxiliaries, presumably). He said that a brief gun battle had ensued and a man was injured on each side. He said the rebels believed they had been attacked by the Pearson brothers and my father, and this was the reason for the brothers being murdered. There are some pointers that suggest that this affray had taken place in the evening, perhaps when light was fading and the enemy not easily identified. My father did not mention this incident but spoke of a few disturbances which took place in the evenings immediately prior to the murders of the two boys and after the family had retired indoors. These took the form of shots being fired and some shouting. My father and the Pearson family believed this activity was created deliberately to intimidate the members of the household. As I have said before, the I.R.A. did not take kindly to being caught unawares, and when this happened, cast about for "spies and informers". In this case, tragically, they didn't have far to look.

More recently, an account from a nationalist point of view has appeared in a book dealing with the history and folklore of the area. It is worthy of some comment. The brief gun battle, with injuries on both sides, is described. I have since spoken with the author. He knew and spoke frequently with a number of the men who were involved with the felled tree affair who told him that the confrontation took place after darkness fell, at midnight to be precise. In these circumstances, identification of attackers would be well nigh impossible. I should also state that none of the Pearsons, or my father, suffered any kind of injury, prior to the killing of Dick and

Abe. This account claims that the battle took place as the tree was being felled, and not later when it was being manned as a barricade. There is an extraordinary claim that after the incident it was discovered that British army officers were with the Pearsons on the particular night. A few people hinted that Matilda, a strikingly good-looking girl, was attracting the attentions of an officer from the Crinkill garrison at Birr, but I have been unable to confirm this in any way. My father told me that on one occasion a British army officer came pushing a motor-cycle up the avenue. He requested, and was given some petrol, before continuing on his way. I am not sure if, in the eyes of the "freedom fighters" this incident alone would be construed as a capital offence, they to be judge, jury and executioner. I must point out again, the British military was not at war with the I.R.A., or *vice versa*. In calling it a "Police War", the British Government described most accurately the folly and tragedy of its own making.

There is a further claim, unsubstantiated, that incriminating material was intercepted in the mail. One is tempted to say, "they would say that, wouldn't they". I have already pointed out that historians have ascertained that Protestants were loath to give information to the authorities, and where this did occur, it was much more likely to come from Catholics.

The account goes on to describe the "flying column" coming to the paddock where haymaking was in progress. A known "British army officer" is described fleeing the scene and making his get-away, in spite of being followed and fired on several times. I think if my father were alive today, he would be amused to learn how quickly he had risen from the ranks. Like the Pearsons, he was just a farm boy, with no connection whatever to the military. In one respect, perhaps, this was unfortunate. How welcome that army pension would have been to tide us over the bleak years of our ill advised and misconceived "economic war" with Britain (1932-38).

The author goes on to describe the courage of Richard and Abraham, as they faced their executioners. The tone and implication is of belligerents in our "glorious war of independence", who, though on the wrong side and in the presence of death, accepted their fate without protest. As I have just said, they were two farm boys, who a few short minutes earlier had been making hay in a field. While I do not doubt their stoicism, there is no mention that on the first barrage of dumdum rounds to the groin, for pity's sake, they did what we all would have done. They turned their backs and took the remaining fire to the buttocks first, and then to the back, as they began to fall. How succinctly the evidence of Dr. Woods makes clear the horror. Few heroics here, I fear.

I asked Mr. Mitchell if the Pearsons had become isolated from their Catholic and, indeed, Protestant neighbours. As we have seen they were not members of the Anglican (Church of Ireland) faith, which at that time, had been 10% of the Irish population, but because of widespread persecution, was diminishing rapidly. As we have seen also, they belonged to a minority Protestant dissenting sect, known as the "Nameless House Church", "Cooneyites" etc. which my informants referred to as "Dippers". Mr. Mitchell assured me there was no isolation. The Catholic family of Mr. Jack White, mentioned in Dave's letter, was particularly close to the Pearsons. I wished to interview members of this family, only to learn that they had long since departed the area, whereabouts unknown. The Pearsons were sociable people he said, great ramblers, i.e. fond of visiting and receiving friends and neighbours, a widespread practice in Ireland at the time. A few people described the young men as being "wild". This was an indication of their high spiritedness, no more. Like any young people they attended parties, dances and frequent concerts, which, at that time, were held in aid of the Red Cross. There was a friendship with a Dr. Hitchcock, a Church of Ireland clergyman, who ministered from Kinnity, 1903-1923. He was the father of the distinguished film director, Rex Ingram, whose films include *The Four Horses of the Apocalypse* (which made Rudolph Valentino a star), and *The Prisoner of Zenda*, among others.

Mr. Mitchell said that, four days after the event, Mrs. Susan Pearson was brought to a house in Kinnity, where a number of men was paraded before her for identification. It should come as no surprise that, as the raiders were masked, she failed to identify any of the men. He also stressed that the Pearson family displayed no bitterness or bigotry as a result of their great loss. He spoke of the very many Catholics who expressed their revulsion to their Protestants neighbours at what had happened, but who, otherwise, because of the prevailing atmosphere, kept their opinions to themselves.

The story of the Pearsons does not end at Coolacrease, and for a time, at least, their fate was closely bound to that of my own family. If you like I would be only too happy to let you have this information, interspersed with the usual delays. I confess to a selfish element to all this. My problem is that I have the information, most of it going back to 1981, in "bits and scraps" all over the place. The discipline of writing to you is compelling me to get it all into decent order at last.

Kind regards,
Alan.

CHAPTER NINE

O Liberté! O Liberté!
Que de crimes on
commet en ton nom!

Mme. Roland

Hello Yvonne,

After the tragedy of Coolacrease the fate of the Pearson family is, to begin with, closely allied to that of my own. But let me speak of my father first. After a few weeks asylum at Tullamore R.I.C. barracks he was spirited away to relatives in the north of Ireland. His father and sister, living in the Queen's County, had learned of the deaths and burning from newspaper reports but had received no news whatever of my father. His first cousin,

Frank Stanley, told me that as a young lad of fourteen he recalled my grandfather coming to his father in great distress. Frank recalled his exact words. "Can happen poor Willie is shot." Finally after a three week interval a postcard arrived from the North. The post was still being intercepted. "Your parcel arrived safely", was the simple code.

I believe my father remained five or six months in the North, long enough to learn of people who called themselves "Loyalists", carrying out atrocities against innocent Catholics, which in a few cases, in horror, emulated the Coolacrease outrage. The worst of these occurred on the 24th March, 1922. Five men, poorly disguised as Constabulary, smashed in the hall door of the home of Mr. Owen McMahon at one o' clock in the morning. He was a prosperous publican of North Belfast. He, his five sons and a barman, were lined up in the sitting room and shot. One son, shielded by the bodies of his loved ones, survived this terror. My father lamented these miseries.

Meanwhile, my grandfather Henry, fearing for my father's life, made plans to sell his farm in the Queen's County and purchase the "Folly" farm, Newchurchwest, near Usk in Monmouthshire, South Wales. He travelled there with his daughter May (Mary), his niece Bessie

(Elizabeth) and some time later was joined by Mrs. Susan Pearson, Sidney and Emily Pearson. I understand that William Pearson Snr. with Dave and the other two girls found a temporary refuge across the border in England. My information on this is sketchy but it seems likely they stayed with a family called Blakemore in Shropshire. I saw the Folly farm in 1983. It was neat and compact and would not have accommodated them all. Here, Susan Pearson was passed off as my grandfather's widowed sister. The reason for this, and for the splitting up of the family, was that the I.R.A. had long tentacles and was quite capable of travelling to other countries, even to Australia, to eliminate its enemies. The family had good reason to continue to be fearful for the lives of Sidney and his father. You will recall that Dave testified that the man who tried to warn the family said the decision had been taken to shoot his three brothers and his father. It was essential therefore, that William Pearson Snr. and Sidney should be separated. Sidney was twenty one years old at this time and one can readily understand that while the perceived deadly threat hung over him, his mother would wish to be at his side permanently. It would be easy for me, with hindsight, to say that with the land secured, and the blood lust satiated, their fears were unfounded. However, they were not in any position to know that.

Close to the "Folly" was "Penyrhoel" farm, c. 200 acres owned by the Welsh ApRhys family (anglicised to Price.) The families became friendly and for a time the youngest of this large family, Doris, "walked out" with Sidney Pearson. She soon transferred her affections to my father whom she married on the last day of 1927. So you see how very nearly I ended up being a kinsman of your husband.

While I was in Wales in 1983 I called on my mother's four brothers, a hardy race of souls who survived into their late eighties and mid nineties. They remembered the Stanleys and Pearsons with great affection and I was astounded to learn that they were still under the misapprehension that Susan was Henry's widowed sister.

A treaty was signed between Britain and an I.R.A. delegation on the 6th December 1921 giving dominion status to twenty-six counties. The new Irish government was beset by problems from the start. Firstly, it had to fight and win a Civil War with those who had opposed the treaty. The war raged from 28th June 1922 to 24th May 1923. Later, with hardly any money in the coffers, there was the question of compensation for the many people, who, like the Pearsons, had lost property. Full compensation was out of the question, but I believe every penny that could be paid was forthcoming. This money enabled the Pearson family, with the exception of Emily who married and settled in England, to make Australia its new home and country.

For the information that follows I am indebted to an Australian teenage schoolgirl, who, for a History Project wrote a prize-winning essay based on interviews with Dave Pearson. This occurred about a year before his death on the 25th April 1991.

It appears that Dave and Matilda and perhaps also Emily went out first leaving England on the 27th May 1927. When they became established the rest of the family followed. On disembarking these were met by newspaper reporters. The young student provides a Photostat of a newspaper cutting from *The Melbourne Argus*, which I reproduce below. Unfortunately, at time of writing I am still awaiting confirmation of the date of the newspaper which has become obliterated on the student's copy.

IRISH LOYALISTS TO SETTLE HERE

TWO SONS KILLED BY REBELS IN 1921

Mr. and Mrs. William Pearson and their grown up son and daughter, a former loyalist Irish family, who suffered at the hands of the rebels in

1921, arrived in Melbourne to-day in
the P. and O. Branch Liner Baradine.
When the ship berthed there was
a happy reunion with three other
members of the family - a son and two
daughters - who had migrated to
Australia several years ago and are
now dairying in Gippsland.
The new arrivals will settle here.
Mr. Pearson Senr., hopes to acquire
a property in Victoria.
Mr. Pearson said that he and his
family formerly lived near Birr,
King's County, Ireland, where he had
his own farm. On June 30., 1921
while he and one son were absent in
another County, a rebel band, about
500 [*sic*] strong, swooped down on the
farm house and set fire to it.

SISTER SAW SHOOTING

They seized two sons - one 24 and
the other 18 - who were busy making
hay. Both were stood up against a

wall and shot by a firing squad.
Miss Ethel Pearson, the daughter
who arrived today, saw the shooting.
She and her Mother were alone in
the farm-house when the revels [*sic*] arrived.
The house was burnt to the ground,
and the rebels escaped before the
arrival of the Military. The Pearsons
were sheltered for several days at the
Birr Garrison.
Later Mr. Pearson had a farm in
Suffolk, (Eng.) Compensation for his
loss was fixed at 7800 pounds stg.,
but he received only 3800 pounds stg.,
from the Irish free State government.

A photograph was published with the article. It showed
Mr. and Mrs. Pearson with Ethel and Sidney. It would
seem from this account that Emily did travel to Australia
with Dave and Matilda. If this is the case she returned
soon after and settled down to married life in England,
of which more anon.

"A rebel band of 500 strong." This is certainly a
type-setter's error and one has to assume that William
said that it was 50 strong. You will recall that *The King's*

County Chronicle reported the number at 40. The nationalist *Midland Tribune Newspaper* quoting from the notes of the same reporter recorded 30 armed men. I am inclined to think that this is the more realistic figure, still sufficiently a "sledge hammer" to crush a "fly."

We know, too, that Ethel and her mother were not alone in the house and that there was more than one witness.

The compensation paid for the property amounted to 48.72% of the fixed value.

Our young student gives a concise and clear account of Dave's life in Australia, from his first impression of the land, which, he said, was wild, uncouth, very rough and a far cry from the lush pastures of Ireland. Matilda had acquired a property very quickly and it is likely that she was married by this time. This holding was in Poowong and for a time Dave helped out there. He then worked in the Canefields of northern Queensland but the great depression soon brought this to an end and he returned to Gippsland. After some time another job came up in Dandenong. He worked in an onion processing plant which crushed onions to a powder which was then packed in shakers to be used like salt. Early in 1930 this plant also failed.

However, he had enough saved, perhaps with the

help of his share of the compensation money, to put a deposit on a modest holding of his own. This was at a time when a great many people were leaving the land to avoid further hardship. The writer stressed Dave's independent and determined nature and his confidence that he would see his venture through. It seems the land had to be cleared first by the old and tested slash and burn technique, and stumps "grubbed" out of the earth. This was a happy time as there were neighbours involved in similar work and they all helped each other. In this way the depression brought people together.

After the clearance and laying down of new high quality grass seed came the next problem - rabbits. He "set to" and dug out 3,000 on the first day, thereafter 600 a day for the next few years. He put this to his advantage as the hides were saleable at just a few cents, but with such numbers, this began to mount up. Also with so many of the brutes he was guaranteed never to go hungry, though he admitted there was a limit. He began to build up a herd of milch cows and on the 7th October 1931 he married Kathleen, an Australian girl, who eventually out-lived him.

The Company which bought the milk also supplied the groceries and other needs. They allowed some credit but could always call this in from the milk money.

Dave soon got used to Australian conditions and way of life and really liked it.

His politics were conservative. He liked Prime Ministers Bruce and Menzies and it comes as no surprise that he detested Lang. He remembered the opening of Sydney Harbour Bridge when Lang was preparing, with appropriate pomp and ceremony, to cut the ribbon. He was beaten to it by a Lancer who charged the fabric, slicing it in two, leaving poor Lang with his "hands hanging".

Despite real hardship, Dave never applied for sustenance benefits, always believing in his ability to come through the crisis. He never complained and was always grateful that there was food on the table. He came through the depression with a healthy bank balance and thereafter moved location a number of times, each time improving his circumstances and eventually retired to Packenham (regrettably I do not have the name of the young girl who provided this information).

Kind regards,
Alan.

CHAPTER TEN

There has been an exciting development. A young woman has come across Yvonne's family roots website seeking information on the shooting at Coolacresase. Yvonne has referred her back to me. She is granddaughter to Dave Pearson. Soon we are shooting e-mails back and forth. Questions, questions, she to me and I to her. She speaks movingly of her great love for her grandfather and how she still misses him dearly. She speaks of his sense of humour and how she could coax him, occasionally, to speak in the old Irish way. "Aah, and what would you want me to be saying, girl?" with perfect Irish lilt. She tells of how, as a child, he brought her mushrooming and was not averse to taking her to steal a few apples from nearby orchards. She notes that he hardly ever spoke of Ireland to her, and never of the troubles. When she indicated that she would like to go to Ireland some day, he urged her to save her money and buy a house instead. She did make it to Ireland, eventually, visiting Coolacrease and Killermogh, in 1993. Dave had passed away the previous year.

I feel the beginnings of a new and real friendship here.

Hello Yvonne,

Early in 1928 my father returned to Ireland with his young Welsh bride. May was already married and shortly afterwards my father's cousin Bessie married my Mother's brother Elias. Their children, above all our Welsh relations, were special as we were both first and second cousins. As we have seen too, 1928 was close to the time that the Pearsons, in stages, were moving to Australia. Henry had purchased a home and 70 acre holding for the newly weds in the townland of Quinagh, near Carlow town. A pleasant enough location, my wife and I are resident here to this day.

Apart from early messages to say they had arrived and so on, communications seem to have ceased from this time. I suppose none of them was a great letter writer, though my father was capable of writing an interesting and well constructed missive when required to do so.

In 1951 my father learned from his sister May the address of Emily who was married and settled in England. The previous year, on the 12th January, the 21 year old beautiful and lively older daughter of May and husband Echlin died unexpectedly of a tubercular illness. The disease had been rampant, cutting great swathes through the country's youth, and the Authorities were only beginning to take control of the situation. My father wrote to Emily enclosing some "snap-shots". What follows is a transcript of her wonderful reply. Her letter is undated.

Mongoha,
Stowupland Rd.,
Stowmarket,
Friday.

Dear Willie,

It surely was a pleasant surprise hearing from you with all your family news and how glad I am that you wrote, as it is such a pity to drift out of one another's lives, with all our families have experienced together. A great deal of water has flowed under the mill since last we saw you and I still have a soft spot for Mon. S. W. Well Willie, do let me begin to congratulate you on being the father of 8, you certainly are more prolific than any of us, I being the worst of the lot. Two efforts and unlucky both times so gave it up as a bad job. We, however, are not desolate, as we adopted a baby girl. She is now starting school and we find her grand company. Now one other thing. I don't think how anyone can manage to look like Doris and still be the mother of eight. She looks to be a girl of 24 or 25. Please send the recipe along. You certainly know how to pick 'em. Yes, of course, I did know Echlin and I am sorry to hear they have lost a daughter. As you say it is an awful blow. Please convey my love and sympathy to them both. I suppose you are all farming and quite prosperous folk. I hope so. How lucky you were to miss the war years here. They were pretty grim. I daresay you know Ken is a corn merchant with a flourishing business and we have a farm of about 205 acres, we live in a bungalow on the edge of the small town of Stowmarket, but of course Ken has to work hard and the gentlemen of Whitehall relieve you of any surplus cash. I do miss my people. Australia is so very far away, but it hasn't quite the same pull since my mother died about three years ago. Father had died 12 years previous to that, and just fancy your father being dead 20 years. How the years do fly!!!

Well now for a little family news. I shall begin with Tilly. She has two children, a girl - who got married about six weeks ago - and a boy. They have retired from farming (T. and W. I mean) and have gone in for house property and are living in a seaside town. Ethel also married an

Irishman and they have one little girl. Go in [*sic*] for house property too and Albert has a good job at Mackays, Sunshine. Dave has done very well in farming and at one time he tried his hand at being a land agent, but didn't do so well, so gave it up, but I think he is now in town studying with a firm to become a land agent, this seems to be his ambition as far as I can gather. He married an Australian girl and they have two sons. Is still as wild as the hare that went mad in March. Now we come to Sydney, he married a girl from these parts (Eng.) and they have two children - a girl and boy. They still live on the farm Dad bought for him, it is a lovely place and I am told he is very rich. Years ago he had electricity laid on because it came right past his door and the government also ran a main city road through his farm and he got a packet for that. I often wonder why they do not come to England for a trip as Vera's parents are now getting old and would love to see her again.

Well I hope I haven't bored you with this long recital of family affairs, but I Promise not to do it again. When you write again, as I hope you will do tell me how and where Bessie and Elias are. I hope they are doing all right. Doris's family too, I hope her parents are still living and well. They wouldn't be so very old. I daresay you do take a journey to Mon. sometimes, but there I can guess a family of eight must keep you fully occupied, but some of them are beginning to do nicely for themselves. Well I had better dry up or you will have to take a day off to read this so will conclude by wishing you and yours all the very best.

Kindest regards,
Your fond cousin,
Emma.

P. S. Haven't got any recent "snaps" at the moment but hope to send one or two later.
E.

They were not cousins, though they always referred to each other as such. I learned this in the early sixties when I queried it with my father. He said there was no connection apart from a few intermarriages between members of the wider families. The sobriquet "cousin" was a measure of the longstanding closeness between the two families.

What a delightful letter. The strong Irish idiom is there throughout. Irish siblings with Irish spouses. Emma knows who she is and speaks from the heart.

Kind regards,
Alan.

CHAPTER ELEVEN

More excitement. Yvonne and I have moved on to the stage of a few, "chatty asides", family details and so on. In one of these I dropped the name and address of Ethel Pearson's daughter, distant cousin of her husband Jack. Incredibly, they live just a few miles apart in the same district of Melbourne.

Dave's granddaughter, her name is Kaylene, is mother to two small boys. She asks me how soon I expect to complete and publish my e-mail "essays". I tell her it's a slow process, but I'm getting there. I express a concern I have had for some time. In attempting to tell it as it is, I may have been guilty of some indelicate intrusion into the lives of the family in Australia. Kaylene assures me that I need have no worries on that account. She says they are looking forward to the finished product. What is of most importance to the family is to know that there are people in Ireland who genuinely care, and will want to know and read of the fate of the Pearsons of Coolacrease.

Hello Yvonne,

After Emma's letter, I can find no evidence of communication between my father and the Pearsons for twenty one years. If the promised "snaps" ever arrived, I have not seen them. However, nine years later, my sister Hilary and her husband Ernest, settled in Geelong, Victoria, immediately after they married in June 1960. In October of that year, they contacted Ethel, who lived closest to them, in Melbourne. Her address had been furnished by my father's sister, May. Ethel's husband Albert was a house agent, and also owned a waste disposal business. Their only child, a daughter named Doris, was still with them at that time.

Ethel made them welcome and altogether "at home", and on leaving, extracted a promise from Hilary that she would come again for a longer stay. The promise was fulfilled eventually in 1962 with Hilary's sixteen month old son. Ernie drove his family up to Melbourne and while there, visited Matilda (Tilly), who was recovering from a foot injury in Prince Henry Hospital. Both were bowled over by the strong presence and personality of this lady. She was extremely bright, quick witted and jolly. She was tall and elegant and retained remarkable good looks. She made a strong and lasting impression. It was Tilly, the eldest girl who, prior to the shootings, asked the raiders "what was the reason for their action in burning the house?" She was aged twenty-three.

Hilary's stay with Ethel was memorable, in that kindness and attention were lavished on her and the babe from all sides. She continued to see Ethel at one to two year intervals, to the end, an end which, regrettably, was presaged by one of the dreadful debilitating diseases that so frequently afflict the elderly. Confusion was manifest at first, building later to paranoia. She once told Hilary that De Valera had stayed in their house, dressed as a woman. This would be remarkable, if true, but highly unlikely. Then sadly, near the end, she fixed padlocks to her doors and whispered dark warnings of the imminent arrival of the I.R.A.

My father visited her on his first trip to Australia in 1972, when the disease had already gained a stranglehold. At this time, too, he attempted to contact Sid, but was thwarted when the car they were travelling in broke down on route. Circumstances also prevented him from seeing Dave on this occasion.

Hilary and husband Ernie first came into contact with Dave in 1962-63, and thereafter, at regular intervals. They liked him enormously from the start. They humorously referred to him as a "bushy." This was to indicate only his love of things natural, and of open spaces, not at all any hint of lacking in sophistication. He enjoyed a beer and loved to attend the races. He indulged a risqué humour, which he shared with Ernie, though never within earshot of Hilary. At their retirement home, which he shared with his wife Kathleen at Packenham, he would invite Ernie to inspect his fruit and vegetable garden. This was a splendid affair that supplied all their needs, and enabled Kathleen to make the most flavoursome and varied preserves. It was not, to any degree of purpose, to the garden they retired. It was, rather, to the garden shed, where Dave kept an ample supply of his favourite Australian beer.

Because of the constraint of distance, they saw less of Sidney than the others. Nevertheless, over the years they met him a number of times. He possessed all the positive traits of his siblings, and was, perhaps different only in that he continued to take his Christianity very seriously. You will recall that according to Dave's testament he was absent with his father, at a "Christian Convention" on the day of the shooting. Hilary, who was a smoker at that time, abstained when he was around. Nothing was said. She just felt that it was right to do so. In the early years of their acquaintance, Dave once had cause to spend a weekend at Sid's farm. His visit coincided with some active prayer sessions, at Sid's home, with a number of likeminded people. This was not altogether to Dave's liking. In a neat piece of "Hiberno-English speak" he confessed to Hilary, "Aah sure they drove me mad."

It was during my father's second visit in 1974 that Hilary arranged for Sid and Dave, with their respective spouses, to visit in Geelong, almost fifty three years after they had last seen each other. The meeting was, as you would expect, most cordial. No mention whatever was made of Coolacrease. Still, how I would like to have been the "fly on the wall." Hilary has confirmed for me that in her numerous meetings with various Pearson family members, the subject of Coolacrease, in any form did not arise. Once there was a hint. Dave said to Hilary, "we were very fond of your father. He stayed with us you know." There was, of course, the one exception, when I asked Hilary in 1981, to approach Dave for a written statement. When he handed her the document, finally, in 1983 he said, I don't want to hear or speak of this affair again, as long as I live. For a moment, Hilary felt she had been an intruder. The real intruder was safely tucked in bed some twelve and a half thousand miles away. In spite of this, Hilary later had a strong sense that the making of the statement had been a catharsis for Dave, a cauterising of a deep inner wound.

In the summer of 1975 Dave and Kathleen visited Emma at Stowmarket in England. Later, with Emma, they flew to Ireland, where Hilary and Ernie were holidaying. They all met at "Carrig" (house), in the village of Killincarrig, County Wicklow. This was the home of my brother John (Jack), and his wife, Patricia. It was also my father's new address, as he occupied a flat adjacent to Carrig at that time. They were congregated there on the day that De Valera was interred. Someone mentioned to Dave that De Valera had died. Very quietly, and without rancour he said, "it's a pity he was ever born."

Within days, Sid also flew in, having come directly from Australia. Together they visited some relatives, and one afternoon drove to Kinnity. This was only after Hilary had assured them they would be quite safe to do so, that things were different then. They went to Cadamstown first, then, drove out to where the entrance to Coolacrease once stood. At that time it was still just recognisable, today it is the site of a modern bungalow. They continued slowly up the road, until they came to that point where the remains of the stricken house stand most colossally, broodingly, still dominating the landscape. This was no classical structure, nor did its design grace the architect's drawing board. Yet, in a few respects, this remarkable vernacular pile can be compared to the formal and very grand "Cuba Court" at Bannagher, some twenty six miles distant, and now, sadly, also in ruin. Our foremost architectural historian, Maurice Craig, describes Cuba as a "splendidly masculine house." The same surely can be said of Coolacrease. No womankind was engaged in its planning, otherwise, like Cuba Court, such massive scale would not have been employed. The sometimes restriction of having to traverse one room of this five bay structure in order to gain access to another, would also have been avoided.

Without exchanging words the two men lingered for an interval, then, drove slowly away.

The weeks of their Irish summer holiday sped happily by. My father waved a fond last farewell to his "cousins", and they winged their paths to their respective homes. Only Tilly and Ethel never made it back to Ireland. All were elderly. All still had a part to play. Then, after a span of years, my father was the first to go, followed in quiet succession by the others, till none was left.

Let Hilary have the last word. "These were the best

people" she said. "To be their friend was a privilege. They harboured no bitterness. They were generous to a fault. They were intelligent, industrious and resourceful. They loved life. They loved to laugh. They were brave people. They were gentle people."

Kind regards,
Alan.

CHAPTER TWELVE

…all decent Irish men.

The man Donnelly

Hello Yvonne,

Over the years a triad of signals has filtered, faintly, through the divide. These seemed to suggest unease, even acknowledgment, by certain people, that a mistake had been made, an injustice committed.

The first was told to me by the late Eric Pearson, of Athy, County Kildare. In the early years of the new "Free State", he had some business to conduct at the Police Station in Rathdowney. Eric understood, by the grapevine, that the police sergeant had been one of those who had made the raid on Coolacrease. A great many of the wild young men of the I.R.A. had subsequently served with distinction in the Police and Army. There was some form filling involved, and when Eric spoke his surname the Sergeant's eyebrows raised. Eric threw caution to the winds. "Yes, I'm related," he said. He was a second cousin. "Those boys were shot in the wrong", the sergeant said.

The second occurred c. 1935, when a journeyman "saw doctor" called to my father at Carlow. My father had felled some trees and was pleased to use his services. Afterwards, he engaged the man in conversation, and asked him where he came from. The man named a townland, my father was familiar with it, near Cadamstown. He probed. "Wasn't there some trouble, nearby, back in '21?" "Oh yes", the man replied, "the Pearson boys. Of course, it was a mistake you know. They should never have been shot." My father took solace from this testament, and never neglected to mention it in his recollection.

More recently, Mr. Tom Mitchell, of Kinnity, was enjoying a drink in a pub there. The newscaster on T.V. announced the latest gruesome murder by the Provisional I.R.A., in Northern Ireland. This was 1981-82. An elderly man, called Donnelly, with whom Tom was on friendly terms, though not in his company, became emotional and spoke loudly. He condemned the

"Provisionals", who shamed all decent Irishmen, and whose campaign was one of heartless murder. He then recalled the shooting of the Pearson boys, and declared this to be no less heinous. It was understood that this man had never been a member of the I.R.A., though he had a brother, who was active.

For the fast diminishing minority community, there was to be only one course of action. That was to take the advice of their leaders, and "keep their heads down." With bleak irony, the upcoming Civil War was to prove a form of "letting off the hook," for this people. So much bitterness was generated among former "comrades in arms", that the spotlight of attention on the minority was reduced, though not removed.

For the relatives, friends and the community to which the Pearsons belonged, and from whom their Unionist identity had been forcibly removed, there was to be no redress, no Calvinistic retribution or requital. Yet, deep in the psyche of a number of these people there was the overwhelming assurance that the wicked could not go unpunished. And so, to comfort themselves, they fostered a myth. The myth told them that all of the leading perpetrators of this murderous act, themselves, shortly thereafter, came to sudden and violent ends. There were a few variants as to how this, supposedly, came about. The one favoured by my father speaks of armed occupants of a lorry, speeding by the blackened shell of Coolacrease, amid much whooping, cheering and discharging of weapons into the air. The vehicle careers out of control and all are killed instantly.

In some quarters the myth is still alive and well, when I was making enquiries in 1982.

I began this narrative, by describing my father's flight from the Queen's County, in the summer of 1921. Now I must re-visit that time and place.

Before the institution of landlordism could be eliminated finally in 1903, various efforts, by governments, since 1860, had been made to accommodate tenant rights. Nothing could have prepared Lord Landsdowne, who owned extensive lands in the Queen's County, for a revolt that blew up in his face, in the fading years of the nineteenth century.

The revolt was centered on the tiny village of Luggacurran, and its leader was the Roman Catholic curate, of that parish. As a boy, he had seen his family evicted onto the road, and he nurtured a rabid resentment of landlords and landlordism. His senior, the Parish Priest, was indisposed with a serious illness. The curate, loosed from shackles of authority, had free rein. He used his pulpit to incite his flock to withhold payment of rents to Landsdowne. Landsdowne was a model landlord, and his tenants knew they had no cause to be aggrieved. However, fear of "the cloth" was a more deadly affair than the awesome esteem of the landlord. When a number of moieties failed to materialise, Landsdowne was compliant. He offered more time. He offered reductions. Eventually, when he found himself fighting a cash flow problem, he evicted the tenants. In anticipation of this the curate had built a "wooden village", i.e. timber shacks to house the evicted families. These were situated in a field adjacent to his church and the village. Landsdowne too had plans. He advertised for new tenants, and these were not slow in coming. Among them were four Stanley brothers from Rathdowney; my Grandfather Henry, William, James and Robert. If they paused for a moment to betray an iota of compassion for the former tenants ("these people thought they should have the land for nothing"), no rumour of the event has come my way. What did cause them no little concern was that they were required to pay all of the outstanding rentals, before moving in.

Well, the new settlers remained, and were known as "planters" to those whose neighbours they became, and "land grabbers" to people who despised them for what they had done. Eventually, most of the former tenants were re-settled, and peace restored. An upheaval like the full-scale rebellion that held sway in 1921, was bound to revive old enmities. I was inclined to assume that this was the reason my father had been banished from his area. On closer examination, in 1982, I found this was not the case. At a later date, during the Civil War, William Stanley's family was made to suffer, apparently, on that account.

With the exception of my Grandfather, all three brothers had large families, so while my father had only one sibling (sister), he had many cousins living in the area. It was one of these, Frank Stanley, who confirmed what others had told me, and he also expanded on the information. He was aged fifteen, in 1921. Frank spoke candidly. He said that my father used to keep company with a number of young men of the area. Like him, they were all sons of "planters". They were Francis Mullins, whose people had come from Scotland, James Kavanagh who later married Frank's sister Violet, George Sythes and Edward Stanley, son of William. Edward later rose to senior rank in the Canadian Mounted Police. All were in possession of a pistol of one kind or another. My father's was an ancient horse pistol, still in working order. They liked, Frank said, "to play at soldiers", to hone their target skills, and indulge in bravado, and naive talk. Where did they get the small arms? The authorities had ordered that all arms be surrendered. The I.R.A., in raids on households all over the country, had accounted for the balance. I don't know the answer. It is, to be sure, an immutable law of the misery of the human condition, that where there is armed conflict, there will be a surfeit of arms. What is certain is that they were held illegally.

Frank described an incident that revealed the extent of their amateurish naivety. One Sunday afternoon, they were "fooling about" at the dairy door of Kavanagh's farm. A weapon discharged, accidentally, causing superficial wounds to one of the group. It could so easily have caused a fatality.

A decent young Catholic neighbour, named Jack Crowley wanted to be part of the group. They rejected him, unkindly, declaring him to be a spy.

The ringleader was Kavanagh. He had the most status, because he owned a motorcycle, and also had the advantage of having two or three very pretty sisters. He liked to go careering along the country lanes on his machine, discharging his weapon skyward as he went.

Then, unwittingly, Kavanagh's mother committed the most foolhardy act of the lot. At Sunday Matins, she espied two handsome young Englishmen, auxiliary

Police Cadets, and invited them home for lunch. They were in Ireland to boost the Royal Irish Constabulary, thereby promoting the British Government's concept of a "Police War", to deal with a "criminal conspiracy". The Government felt restrained by public opinion from using full military strength to put down what was, in reality, an all-out armed rebellion. One of the unfortunate side effects of this myopic policy was that over four hundred and fifty Royal Irish Constabulary men were murdered by the I.R.A. "Political killings", we are told nowadays, as if this made a difference. My father saw two of them shot down in the street in Kinnity. They were twenty-five year old constable Edward Doran of Wexford and twenty-three year old constable John Dunne of Galway. Their killers skulked behind the R.C. Church before "striking their blow for Ireland". For a time it was thought they had used a ladder, which Tom Mitchell had been using to clear the gutters, to make their getaway. Tom, himself was briefly under suspicion. "Two fine young Irish lads", my father bewailed. In any case, Mrs. Kavanagh said she felt sorry for the two young English men, so far from home. I suspect she may have been disheartened by the coterie of gun-toting yokels lounging about her place. There may well have been the expectation of more hopeful bridegroom material for her pretty daughters.

It seems there was more than a social element to their visits to the Kavanagh household. Violet Stanley, Frank's sister, who later married James Kavanagh, told me she overheard them discuss plans to "lift" a young man of the area who was an active I.R.A. member. Violet was aged about thirteen at this time. The young man's name was Martin Byrne. Later, in July 1927 he went on the run from the authorities. It was believed that he was a suspect in connection with the assassination of Kevin O'Higgins, Minister for Home Affairs in the first Free State Government. In the course of the Civil War, O'Higgins had signed warrants for execution by firing squad of seventy-seven Republicans (i.e. those opposed to the treaty). Violet went immediately to the Byrne household to warn them. A sister grasped her by the arm and demanded, "who told you? Who told you?" Violet used all her strength to disengage and ran as fast as she was able. I asked her what prompted her to warn Byrne. "He was a neighbour", she said, "a lovely fellow. He played with us kids. He was a handsome lad. I suppose I was partly in love with him." A few years earlier, in happier times, my father and Martin had hunted rabbits on the Black Mountain. They switched firearms. Later my father told me he may well have shot rabbits with the weapon that was used to slay O'Higgins. This may not be as bizarre as it seems. The killing of O'Higgins was carried out by an arbitrary twosome. Martin Byrne died of exposure through having to hide out in the open, because the era of "the safe house" was no more. My father, recalling the sport they had enjoyed, deplored the manner of his dying.

If the local brigade (I.R.A.) had tolerated "playing at soldiers", "fraternising with the enemy" was a different matter altogether, one that in many cases exacted the extreme penalty. It was not long until, this "pack of whelps", as Frank described them, got notice to leave. Frank thought the notices arrived by registered post. One wonders if they had special markings, to save the people who were intercepting the mail, from time wasting rifling. Frank believed it was the decency of the Luggacurran people that enabled them to get off so lightly.

The question arises, why did my grandfather, Henry, not exert more control? He was a busy man. His wife had died in 1919. They had undertaken to rear two nieces, and also to look after two nephews, the Sullivan brothers, during school vacations. Henry continued in this vein. Frank confirmed what I already knew. Henry was illiterate as were his brothers. Even so, he can hardly have been unaware of the events taking place all around him. He was a member of the sectarian Orange Order Society, and it is unlikely he received the correct signals from that quarter. Yet, everywhere I look he has left a legacy of decency and unselfish generosity. The historian, Peter Hart, in his study of the Cork I.R.A., learned how the vast majority of fathers were strongly opposed to their sons' involvement with the I.R.A., but were quite powerless in the face of the general air of rebelliousness. One wonders if my father and his friends were also caught up in this common malaise.

Henry died before I was born, in 1940 and my earliest recollections of my father are as a middle-aged man. His moods varied from the most remarkable perception and wit, to a slough of bleak despair. His pain, compounded by mania, was engendered by loss. In his case, it was the loss of a large portion of his identity. He was an Irishman, who had been born a Briton. An armed conspiracy had robbed him of that privilege, still enjoyed by his English, Welsh and Scottish former compatriots. His Irishness was equally important to him. His language, Hiberno-English, was that shared by the vast majority of his countrymen. He articulated better than most of his peers. In the beginning, at election time, he voted for the "pro treaty" *Fine Gael* party, even making his automobile available for ferrying the old and infirm to the voting booths. With the ever increasing isolationism, and craven confessional approach to political affairs, he soon became disillusioned. When a *Fine Gael* led government took Ireland out of the British Commonwealth in 1949, it was the last straw.

If the "id" of his personality caused no little grief, he cultivated the "ego" with energy. He was popular among his neigbours. He never refused requests to be guarantor for essential purchases, or luxuries such as motorcycles or musical instruments. In one case, for a man whose politics were candidly nationalist, he sponsored the building of a new house.

There is a myriad of recollections. Let me mention just a few. I recall his good-humoured teasing of my mother when she played "Men of Harlech" on the piano. "Always knew she was a Welsh nationalist at heart. There'll be no stopping her now." I recall his fond embrace of welcome for my young Irish bride, whose Gaelic maiden name is *Cait Ní Aimhirgín*. Later, I recall his pride in her achievements, and his exceptional kindness to her to the end.

Occasionally, in the gloaming of my sleep time I journey to him. He graciously invites me in, to where my Mother is waiting. With cups of tea and Welsh cakes, we circle the hearth, and are consoled, for he knows that I comprehend at last.

This is the end, Yvonne. Sometimes I muse on how it might have been had Dick and Abe not met their fate. My father would not have fled, nor later without his Welsh spouse, spawned me into the morass. And, would I forfeit the questionable prerogative of my existence to afford them a second chance??

I am a coward . . .

With most kind regards,
Alan.